THE METRIC SYSTEM

Paul Challen

Crabtree Publishing Company
www.crabtreebooks.com

Author: Paul Challen
Coordinating editor: Chester Fisher
Series editor: Penny Dowdy
Editor: Reagan Miller
Proofreader: Ellen Rodger
Editorial director: Kathy Middleton
Production coordinator: Margaret Amy Salter
Prepress technician: Margaret Amy Salter
Cover design: Samara Parent
Logo design: Samantha Crabtree
Project manager: Kumar Kunal (Q2AMEDIA)
Art direction: Dibakar Acharjee (Q2AMEDIA)
Design: Shruti Aggarwal (Q2AMEDIA)
Photo research: Poulomi Basu (Q2AMEDIA)

Photographs:
123RF: Rolf Klebsattel: p. 14 (bottom center)
Alamy: image100: front cover (center)
Dreamstime: p. 19
Fotolia: Klinger: p. 19; Aaron Kohr: p. 21
Istockphoto: John Cooke: p. 1; Kieran Flynn: p. 20 (top); Ruben Hidalgo:
    p. 11; Kemie: p. 7 (left); Rene Mansi: p. 9; Tyler Olson: p. 20 (bottom);
    Dimitry Romanchuck: p. 21; Terry Wilson: p. 16 (left)
Q2AMedia Art Bank: p. 4, 5, 9, 12–13, 14, 18, 23
Shutterstock: Matt Benoit: p. 14 (bottom right); Steven Coling: p. 10 (left);
    Sonya Etchison: p. 15 (top); Koshevnyk: p. 14 (bottom left); Veniamin
    Kraskov: p. 6; Emin Kuliyev: p. 5; Chepe Nicoli: p. 17; Maglcoven: p. 19;
    Marc Pinter: p. 15 (bottom); Terry Wilson: p. 16 (right), 17; Viktar Ramanenka:
    front cover (bottom right); Michael Rolands: p. 7 (right); Robert Spriggs:
    folio image; Tischenko Irina: p. 10 (right); Anke Van Wyk: p. 19

Library and Archives Canada Cataloguing in Publication

Challen, Paul, 1967-
    The metric system / Paul Challen.

(My path to math)
Includes index.
ISBN 978-0-7787-4352-1 (bound).--ISBN 978-0-7787-4313-2 (pbk.)

    1. Metric system--Juvenile literature. I. Title. II. Series:
My path to math

QC92.5.C43 2009   j530.8'12   C2009-903583-9

Library of Congress Cataloging-in-Publication Data

Challen, Paul C. (Paul Clarence), 1967-
    The metric system / Paul Challen.
        p. cm. -- (My path to math)

    Includes index.
    ISBN 978-0-7787-4352-1 (reinforced lib. bdg. : alk. paper)
    -- ISBN 978-0-7787-4313-2 (pbk. : alk. paper)
    1. Metric system--Juvenile literature. I. Title.

QC92.5.C43 2010
530.8'12--dc22
                                    2009022855

Crabtree Publishing Company

www.crabtreebooks.com   1-800-387-7650

Printed in China/012011/GW20101014

Published in Canada
Crabtree Publishing
616 Welland Ave.
St. Catharines, ON
L2M 5V6

Published in the United States
Crabtree Publishing
PMB 59051
350 Fifth Avenue, 59th Floor
New York, New York 10118

Published in the United Kingdom
Crabtree Publishing
Maritime House
Basin Road North, Hove
BN41 1WR

Published in Australia
Crabtree Publishing
386 Mt. Alexander Rd.
Ascot Vale (Melbourne)
VIC 3032

Contents

A Visit to the Lab

Sam likes to visit his Aunt Lisa at work. Lisa is a scientist. She works in a lab. Lisa has tools to help her **measure** things. She uses a tool to measure how hot or cold something is. She uses different tools to measure how long something is or how heavy something is. Sam wants to help Lisa with her work. So Lisa teaches Sam how to measure.

Aunt Lisa measures many things in the lab.

It All Measures Up

Lisa uses the **metric system** when she measures. People around the world use the metric system to measure. They can share a way of talking about how hot or cold the air is. They use the same words to tell how heavy something is.

Every kind of measuring uses a different tool. Lisa tells Sam about different metric measures. Then they use a tool to practice measuring.

▶ **Thermometers** are tools that measure hot and cold.

Fact Box

You can see metric measurements on things like milk cartons or cereal boxes.

► We can measure how much liquid something holds.

◄ We can measure how long something is.

What Is the Temperature?

Sam asks how to find how hot or cold something is. Lisa shows him a thermometer. The thermometer is a tool to measure **temperature**. Metric thermometers are marked in **degrees Celsius**. The symbol used to show degrees Celsius looks like this: °C.

The thermometer has lines and numbers. Each line stands for one degree. The red colored line in the middle of the thermometer moves up and down depending on the temperature. Lisa measures the temperature of the air. The red line on this thermometer stops at the number 15. So Lisa writes the temperature like this: 15°C.

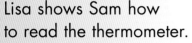

Lisa shows Sam how
to read the thermometer.

9

Some Like it Hot!

Lisa says that low temperatures mean something is cold. Water freezes and turns to ice at 0°C. High temperatures mean something is hot. Water boils at 100°C.

100°C

0°C

Activity Box

What is the outdoor temperature today in degrees Celsius?

Sam checks the temperature of the room. The thermometer reads 23°C. That is a normal temperature for indoors. Sam takes the thermometer outside. It reads 34°C. It is hot out!

▶ When we know the temperature outside, we know how to dress when we go out to play!

°C

50

40   45

30   35

20   25

10   15
                    23°C

0   5

10   5

20   15

The Magic Number 10

The metric system uses a pattern of tens. Learning the pattern makes understanding metric measurements easy!

The word *deca* tells us we have ten of an item. The word *hecto* means ten tens, or 100. Ten hundreds, or 1,000, is called a *kilo*.

kilo	hecto	deca	
1,000 of	100 of	10 of	1

Cut a piece of paper into 10 pieces.
This makes a *deci*, or ten equal parts.

Cut each of your ten pieces of paper into
ten more pieces of paper. You now have
100 pieces of paper. One hundred equal
parts is called a *centi*. If you cut each of
your 100 pieces of paper into ten parts,
you would have 1,000 parts. One
thousand equal parts is called a *milli*.

deci	centi	milli
10 equal parts	100 equal parts	1,000 equal parts

Measuring Up

Lisa shows Sam a **meter** stick. The meter stick measures length.

Sam can use the meter stick to measure the length of the room. But what tool would he use to measure something shorter? Lisa hands Sam a centimeter (cm) ruler. Sam can use the centimeter ruler to measure things such as the length of his fingers, or the length of his shoe. It takes 100 centimeters to make one meter.

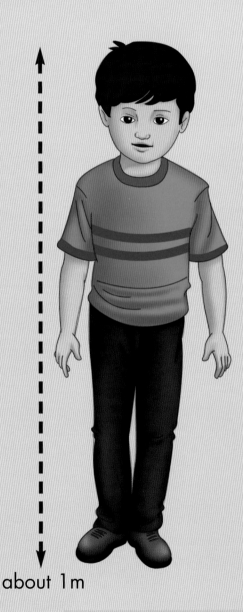

about 1m

Sam stands about a meter tall.

about 1cm

◀ Measure your thumb in centimeters using a ruler. Your thumb is about one centimeter wide.

about 1km

▲ Two laps around the track is about one kilometer in length.

Heavy Stuff!

Lisa hands Sam an empty bottle and a rock. Sam notices that the two objects are about the same size. The bottle is light. The rock is heavy. The rock has more inside of it. It has more **mass**.

Lisa shows Sam a **balance**. A balance is a tool that measures mass. She puts the rock on one side of the balance. She puts weights on the other side. Now the balance is even. The weights show the rock's mass.

The rock has more ▶ mass than the bottle.

A balance measures the mass of the rock.

Fact Box

People have used balances for thousands of years. Balances are still used to measure mass today.

Heavy and Light

Lisa measures mass in **grams** (g). A dime weighs about one gram. Some things have even less mass. Imagine cutting a dime into 1,000 pieces. Just one of those pieces weighs about one milligram (mg). Now that is light!

Some things have a lot of mass. A kilogram (kg) is 1,000 grams. A brick weighs about one kilogram. Lisa can measure Sam's mass in kilograms.

▶ Sam weighs 35 kilograms

Activity Box

Find the mass of a pencil. Use a balance to find the weight in grams.

The coin is measured in grams. The brick is measured in kilograms.

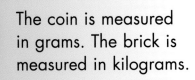

Liquids

Lisa gives Sam a measuring cup. Then she asks Sam to fill it with water. The measuring cup holds one **liter** (L).

▲ This measuring cup measures liquid.

Lisa uses a dropper to show Sam a milliliter. Sam remembers learning the word *milli*. So he knows that 1,000 milliliters make one liter. Lisa asks Sam how much a kiloliter (kl) would be. Sam says kilo is 1,000 liters. That is a lot of water! A bathtub is too small to hold a kiloliter!

▶ This water bottle holds one liter.

This water dropper gives out one drop of water at a time. Each drop is about one milliliter of water.

The water in the pool could be measured in kiloliters.

Glossary

balance A tool used for measuring mass

degrees Celsius The metric measurement for temperature (°C)

gram The metric unit for measuring mass (g)

liter The metric unit for measuring liquid (L)

mass How much material is inside something

measure To find the temperature or size of an object

meter The metric unit for measuring length (m)

metric system Measurements based on Celsius degrees, meters, grams, and liters

temperature How hot or cold something is

thermometer A tool used for measuring temperature

kilo	hecto	deca		deci	centi	milli
1,000 of	100 of	10 of	1	10 equal parts	100 equal parts	1,000 equal parts

Index